Live and Learn!

Basic American Idioms *for* ESL Students

Compiled by J. L. Angelini

ACKNOWLEDGEMENTS

My sincere thanks to the Literacy Volunteers of Morris County, New Jersey for training me to become an ESL tutor, to Lyubov Kovaleva for being a wonderfully patient and diligent student and my inspiration, and to Robin Timpson for her eagle-eyed proofreading and helpful suggestions.

Introduction

Let's not beat around the bush. Learning and remembering idioms and idiomatic phrases are a tall order for ESL students. There are more English idioms than you can shake a stick at — as there are in most languages. Learning them all won't be a piece of cake, but if you keep your shirt on and your chin up, and give it your best shot, you will find that this book will help do the trick.

There are eight idiomatic phrases in the above paragraph. Did you recognize any of them? Now, here is the same paragraph with the idioms replaced:

Let's be clear. Learning and remembering idioms and idiomatic phrases are challenging for ESL students. There are thousands of idioms in English — as there are in most languages. Learning them all won't be easy, but if you are patient and determined, and try hard, you will find that this book will help you succeed.

There is no question that for any language student, idioms can be difficult and confusing to understand and remember. But, they are also a practical and fun means of expressing oneself in a richer and more colorful way. And, as most native speakers of a language tend to use idiomatic phrases rather than simple words to express themselves in conversation, it is important for language students to add as many of these phrases as possible to their vocabulary.

A book, such as this one, is only one step on the road to acquiring an adequate knowledge of these phrases, and its aim is to give ESL students a basic list of popular idioms — idioms that the ESL student is most likely to hear in common daily use. In order to expand their vocabulary, students would be wise to listen carefully for idiom use in the conversations of the native speakers around them. This includes TV and radio programs, as well as news broadcasts, and movies. Here are two examples of the general way idioms are used:

After a recent blizzard in New York City, a reporter on a local news broadcast said that getting around the City in all the snow wouldn't be *"a walk in the park"* — meaning, it wouldn't be easy. And, when an 84-year-old celebrity made public his engagement to a 24-year-old woman, it was unsaid but clear that he was *robbing the cradle* — which has nothing to do with actually stealing a baby from its bed.

To help the student more easily learn and remember them, the idioms in this book are listed in related groups: food, animals, parts of the body, sports and action, numbers and money, clothing and household items, natural elements, colors, and miscellaneous. There are also practice exercises for each section.

Finally, it is hoped that you will have fun using this book as you improve your language skills. After all, learning a language shouldn't be *all work and no play.*

Notes:

Many idiomatic phrases include verbs. Remember to correctly conjugate the verbs in the idiomatic phrases which include them.

Example: Idiom = *smell* a rat

Sentence use = When he found his desk drawer open, Bob *smelled* a rat. (past tense)

The idioms listed sometimes include the words *one, one's, someone, someone's,* or *something* in parentheses. In usage, these words are to be replaced with an appropriate noun or pronoun.

Example: Idiom = *(one's)* goose *is* cooked

Sentence use = *Jimmy's* goose *was* cooked once his mom read the note from his teacher.

Some idioms allow for variations in their syntax or word order while others do not.

Example: Idiom = wrap (someone) around (one's) finger

Variation = (someone) *is wrapped* around (one's) finger

Certain idioms are open to variations in the words used as well. Where appropriate, some word variations are included in the idioms list, such as: use *(one's)* head / noggin / noodle / nut. This indicates that any one of the four words, head or noggin or noodle or nut, would be acceptable to use.

Have fun with the idioms you learn. English, like most languages, is constantly evolving. As new words, especially slang words, become incorporated into everyday English, they will also be included in popular idioms and lead to the formation of new idioms.

Contents

Chow Down

Pies and cakes, eggs, fish and turkeys. Delicious! The idioms in this section might make you hungry, but they are only *food for thought*.

food for thought
something to think about

> Inez has been given some *food for thought*: she can accept a promotion at work or she can use her financial aid to go back to school full time.

from soup to nuts
including everything, as in a full meal

> We like going to the local flea market most weekends. They have everything there — *from soup to nuts*.

(one's) bread and butter
that which gives (one) a regular income

> Now that you have finished school, you have to find some way to earn your *bread and butter*.

butter (someone) up
to praise or flatter (someone) too much

> The boss had a lot of nice things to say about you
> at the meeting this morning. Is he trying to *butter*
> you *up* so he can give you more work?

take (something) with a grain of salt
to not believe something completely

> Bob tends to lie — or at least to stretch the truth
> — so you might want to *take* what he's telling you
> about this financial opportunity *with a grain of salt.*

cry over spilled milk
to think about past misfortunes

> I'm sorry that you missed getting that promotion
> this year, but there's no use *crying over spilled milk.*

lay an egg
to fail or to have (one's) efforts fail

> Everyone expected the latest 3-D movie to be a
> huge success, but audiences everywhere hated it.
> The movie producers *laid an egg* with this one.

put all (one's) eggs in one basket
to risk everything on one project or idea

> Desi *put all* his *eggs in one basket* when he quit his
> steady job and opened a trumpet repair shop.

(have / with) egg on (one's) face
to be embarrassed

> Sanjeev insisted that he knew all his speaking lines
> for the upcoming school play. However, the night
> of the performance he forgot several of them and
> ended up *with egg on* his *face.*

meat and potatoes
the basic parts of something

> Eventually, you will have to learn several computer
> programs for this job. For now, let's get you started
> with the *meat and potatoes* program.

(one's) goose is cooked
(one's) chances are ruined

> Gracie was already being punished by her parents
> for having a bad report card. Then she got sus-
> pended from school. Her *goose is cooked* for sure.

sitting duck
a very easy target

> When you criticized your boss in front of everyone, you made yourself a *sitting duck* for his anger.

cold turkey
to withdraw suddenly from a dependency or addiction

> Haruki stopped smoking cigarettes *cold turkey* last month.

chicken out
to not do something because of great fear

> Franco was going to ask Maria to marry him, but, at the last minute, he *chickened out* and didn't propose.

chicken feed
a small amount of money

> You didn't get paid very much for all the work you did. In fact, what they paid you was *chicken feed*.

bring home the bacon
to work and earn money

> Since Joe lost his job last year, his wife Diana is the only one *bringing home the bacon*.

like a fish out of water
to be totally unfamiliar with (one's) surroundings

> Ravi said he was an experienced short order cook,
> but on his first night working at the diner, he was
> *like a fish out of water* and didn't know what he
> was doing.

spill the beans
to disclose a secret and ruin a plan or surprise

> Who *spilled the beans*
> about Elina's surprise
> birthday party?

as cool as a cucumber
to be very calm

> No matter how busy the diner gets at lunchtime,
> our waitress Rosalind stays *as cool as a cucumber*.

take the cake
to be the most outrageous; to be outstanding

> Yolanda drank too much and danced on the desks
> at the office party last night. She really *took the cake*
> with her wild behavior.

> Yolanda worked very hard on this project; she *takes
> the cake* when it comes to being dedicated.

have (one's) cake and eat it too
to use something but still have it

> While Ann was temporarily unemployed, her parents helped pay her rent. Although she is working again, Ann asked her parents to continue to help her. She wants to *have* her *cake and eat it too.*

a piece of cake / as easy as pie
something that is expected to be easy

> I thought that learning English was going to be *a piece of cake / as easy as pie*, but it is hard.

pie in the sky
an impossibly hopeful goal

> John had big ideas for his future success. Too bad he never became qualified enough to achieve any of those goals. His ideas were all *pie in the sky.*

that's the way the cookie crumbles
that is the way things happen

> Kendra couldn't believe she didn't get that sales contract. She thought it was a certainty. Sometimes *that's the way the cookie crumbles.*

How do you like them / those apples?
What do you think about the current situation?

> Yes, I **was** going to give you the money, but I changed my mind. *How do you like those apples?*

(out of / from) the frying pan and into the fire
free from one problem, but immediately with a worse one

> Joanne quit her last job because of low pay. Her new job pays the same, but her working hours are longer. She went *from the frying pan into the fire.*

what's eating (someone)?
what is bothering (someone)?

> Gosh, Yaphet's very cranky this morning. *What's eating* him?

Chow Down Idioms Exercise

1. Ken works six days a week to _____
   _____ for his wife and four children.

2. Your _____ if you're not
   home from work before 10 o'clock tonight.

3. Painting the bedroom walls was _____
   _____ and we finished sooner than we had expected.

4. When she walked into the classroom as a teacher for the first
   time, Linda felt _____.

5. The boss _____ when he
   forgot to introduce the company president at the meeting.

6. Until he was injured, Rick had been earning his _____
   _____ as a roofer.

7. Carla gave up gambling _____ last year.

8. Did you _____ to her about our
   plans for tomorrow?

9. That business opportunity sounds risky. Maybe you shouldn't
   _____ your _____.

10. There are too many things to review right now. Let's just go
    over the _____ parts.

11. Do you think Sandra will ever become a doctor or is that just
    _____?

12. Okay, so you didn't win this beauty pageant. Don't _____
_____; start preparing for the
next competition.

13. You have such a terrible frown on your face today. _____
_____ you?

14. Desmond was nervous about having to make that important
speech. When the time came, however, he was _____
_____ and did a great job.

15. The car salesmen told you the car only had one owner, but I
would _____ what he said _____.

16. Maria has gone from being in one bad relationship to
another. She keeps jumping _____
_____.

17. Auditioning for a stage play can be nerve-wracking, but
you're very talented, so don't _____.

18. Some movie stars want fame *and* privacy, but they can't
_____ their _____.

19. This job will require you to do many different things, _____
_____, every day.

20. The town council has decided not to extend our contract.
_____?

21. Sharif forgot to bring the file with his presentation on it and
_____ his _____ at the meeting.

22. As he picked his way across the fields, the lone soldier was a _____ for attack.

23. The landscaper bid on two jobs, but only got one. Sometimes in business _____ _____.

24. I can't believe Joel asked for a raise as he is such a poor worker. That guy really _____.

25. Kim was offered the job, but she turned it down because the pay was _____.

26. I'll be happy to give you a ride to work next week. And you don't have to _____ me _____ to get me to do it.

27. Here's some _____: how different would your life be if you were rich?

Answer key begins on page 99

Critters

This bevy of idioms features animals that snarl, bite, and sting, but as captured here, they *wouldn't hurt a fly.*

in the doghouse
> *in trouble*

> Jim got home from work after midnight last night — again. His wife is very upset with him and today he's *in the doghouse.*

dog eat dog
> *extremely competitive*

> Fashion modeling is a *dog-eat-dog* business so you have to be tough as well as beautiful.

dog days
> *the very hot humid days of summer*

> When it's cold and snowing outside, it's hard to remember the uncomfortable *dog days* of summer.

let sleeping dogs lie
to avoid past problems

> Although you had a problem working with Jessica
> in the past, we expect you to *let sleeping dogs lie*
> and to work with her on this project.

teach an old dog new tricks
to replace old habits with new ideas

> Mary is 75 years old and has begun
> taking a computer programming
> class. She firmly believes you **can**
> *teach an old dog new tricks.*

(one's) bark is worse than (one's) bite
(one) isn't as bad as (one) sounds

> The boss got angry because that report wasn't
> finished on time, but don't worry. His *bark is*
> *worse than* his *bite.* Just do a better job next time.

the cat got (one's) tongue
to be unable to speak

> Dina had plenty to say when her supervisor left
> the room, but when he came back in and asked her
> what she had said, *the cat got* her *tongue!*

let the cat out of the bag
to disclose a secret

> Who *let the cat out of the bag* about the company
> moving its headquarters to Houston next month?

more than one way to skin a cat
there is more than one answer to a problem

> Fixing this problem won't be easy,
> but, as there is *more than one*
> *way to skin a cat*, let's see if we
> can figure out other ways to do it.

put the cart before the horse
to do things in an unusual or wrong order

> We always eat dessert **after** dinner. Tonight let's
> *put the cart before the horse* and have our dessert
> first!

hold (one's) horses
to be asked to wait

> The children were very excited to see the new
> panda cub, but the teacher told them to *hold* their
> *horses* and wait quietly until they were allowed in.

dark horse
someone about whom little is known; something unknown

> It was expected that Yuri would win the election, but Ivan entered the race as a *dark horse* candidate and won instead.

a bull in a china shop
someone who is very clumsy

> Tina is a small delicate person. It's hard to believe that she is very clumsy and is *a bull in a china shop*.

cash cow
a good source of money

> Juan thought that his pawn shop would be a *cash cow*, but it has cost him more money than he has earned.

get (someone's) goat
to annoy (someone)

> My sister-in-law is usually pleasant to be with, but she really *got* my *goat* the other night at dinner.

(when) pigs fly
never; impossible

> In thirty years, Rob has never invited any of his friends to his house for dinner. If he did, it would be *when pigs fly*.

go whole hog
to do something completely and lavishly

> When he won re-election, the governor *went whole hog* and had a huge victory party.

as the crow flies
the most direct route between two points

> It's only two miles from here to the library *as the crow flies*, but it's four miles by car as you have to drive around a mountain to get there.

eat like a bird
to eat very little

> I knew my son wasn't feeling well. He was very quiet after school and *ate like a bird* at dinner.

kill two birds with one stone
to accomplish two goals with a single action

> Having a tag sale is a great way to *kill two birds with one stone*: you get rid of things you don't want and you make some money.

for the birds
worthless

> That new movie was neither interesting nor entertaining; in fact, it was *for the birds*.

smell a rat
to suspect that something is wrong

> When Monica learned that her husband had
> begun working late with his young female assistant,
> she began to *smell a rat.*

as quiet as a mouse
very quiet

> It was well after midnight when Sam got home
> from work, so he tried to be *as quiet as a mouse*
> when he went into the bedroom.

monkey business
silly or deceptive conduct; mischief

> The teacher had to leave the room for a few min-
> utes and she warned her students not to try any
> *monkey business* while she was gone.

not / never hurt a fly
to be gentle toward everything

> Although he is physically intimidating, Marco is
> a very kind and gentle man who actually would
> *not hurt a fly.*

Critters Idioms Exercise

1. This party was supposed to be a surprise, but someone _____
   _____ and
   spoiled it.

2. Nino won the lottery and, to celebrate, is _____
   _____ with a big party this weekend.

3. Wilfredo's wife hasn't been feeling well, so he has been _____
   _____ around the house.

4. It's easier to enjoy the _____ of summer if
   you live by a beach or lake and can go swimming to cool off.

5. Tom is such _____
   that his wife won't let him near her antique doll collection.

6. This new computer program may have cost a lot of money,
   but I've used it and I think it's _____.

7. If you don't do something romantic for your wife for Valentine's Day, you will definitely be _____.

8. Max says he will quit smoking but only _____
   _____.

9. When the lawyer asked the witness to state what she had
   seen, _____ her _____
   and she was silent.

10. Whenever Julie is at someone's house for dinner, she _____
    _____ in an effort to be polite.

11. Although she _____
    and raised a family before going to college, Pam's new career
    is going well.

12. The boss will be away next week and it's up to you to see that
    there's no _____ while he's gone.

13. Henry was in sales for many years but got tired of the _____
    _____ environment.

14. Tell the crowd at the door to _____ their _____;
    they'll be admitted soon.

15. There's something about this business contract that doesn't
    seem right. I'm going to have my lawyer review it as I _____
    _____.

16. Wanda's home cleaning business has become a real _____
    _____ for her.

17. We don't have to fix the problem this way. There is _____
    _____ and we're
    open to suggestions.

18. Why do you want to stir up trouble again between those old
    enemies? Can't you _____?

19. They went to a new laundromat that also serves coffee and
    bagels and _____
    _____; they got clean clothes while they ate
    breakfast!

20. The company was worried about hiring a retired engineer but soon realized that you **can** _____ _____.

21. Don't you understand? Zoë decided to apply for the same job as you just to _____ your _____.

22. Brad only looks threatening. He would _____ _____.

23. Jaime expected to be promoted easily, but learned that a _____ from another department is also being considered for that opening.

24. You can see the town of Chesterfield across the lake. It's about twelve miles _____, but almost ninety miles by car.

25. Are you afraid to ask LaDonna for help? Don't worry, her _____ her _____. She'll be glad to help you.

Answer key begins on page 101

Every Body

Here, *right under your nose*, are idioms you can really *sink your teeth into*.

head over heels
> *very intense feelings about (someone or something)*

Joanne met Vincent last Saturday and was immediately *head over heels* about him.

use (one's) head / noggin / noodle / nut
> *to use (one's) common sense*

Bill wasn't sure how to fix the lamp, but, by *using* his *head*, he was soon able to figure out what needed to be done.

bury (one's) head in the sand
> *to refuse to face unpleasant news or situations*

Lack of available parking is a big problem for our town. We must stop *burying* our *heads in the sand* and try to resolve this problem.

give (someone) a piece of (one's) mind
to scold very sharply

> What Cheryl did made me so angry, I'd like to *give* her *a piece of* my *mind.*

face to face
in direct communication

> We have had so many conversations on the phone. I'm really looking forward to finally meeting you *face to face.*

turn a blind eye to
to deliberately ignore

> For many years, Rick's wife *turned a blind eye to* his extramarital affairs.

see eye to eye
to agree

> I'm glad we could see *eye to eye* on solving the financial problems of the church association.

all ears
listening completely

> Go ahead. Keep talking. I'm *all ears.*

in one ear and out the other
ignored and having no effect on the listener

> Teenage children often ignore their parents' advice,
> letting it go *in one ear and out the other.*

wet behind the ears
to be inexperienced

> The young auto mechanic we hired
> recently is still *wet behind the ears,*
> but I'm sure he'll improve quickly.

play it by ear
to do something without a plan

> We have no specific plans for our vacation in Paris.
> We're just going to *play it by ear.*

right under (one's) nose
directly in front of (one)

> Nils searched everywhere in his office for his
> favorite pen. He finally found it on his desk — *right
> under* his *nose.*

pay through the nose
to pay unreasonably high prices

> You should wait for a sale before you buy that new
> TV. You'll *pay through the nose* if you buy it now.

keep (one's) nose clean
to stay out of trouble

> The police released the young man with a warning
> to *keep* his *nose clean* in the future.

no skin off (one's) nose
of little importance to (one)

> Personally, I don't care if you like this decision or
> not. It's *no skin off* my *nose* one way or the other.

nose out of joint
to be in a bad mood

> Ooh, Harry's in a nasty mood today. What's put
> his *nose out of joint*?

nose to the grindstone
to work very hard

> That company pays very well because they expect
> you to put your *nose to the grindstone* every day.

cut off (one's) nose to spite (one's) face
   to harm (oneself) through (one's) own mean actions

> Ava spoiled her chances of a promotion when she
> falsely accused a co-worker she dislikes of harass-
> ment. She *cut off* her *nose to spite* her *face.*

keep (one's) mouth shut
   to not reveal confidential information

> I'll tell you what's going on if you
> promise you'll *keep* your *mouth*
> *shut* about it.

leave a bad taste in (one's) mouth
   to leave a bad sense or feeling with (one)

> Raul's first experience leading a public meeting
> was unpleasant and *left a bad taste in* his *mouth.*

put (one's) foot in (one's) mouth
   to say something embarrassing or thoughtless

> Never guess a woman's age unless you like *putting*
> your *foot in* your *mouth.*

sink (one's) teeth into
   to begin a task with great attention or energy

> Francisco was pleased to finally have a project he
> could *sink* his *teeth into* and he happily settled
> down to work.

fight tooth and nail
to fight aggressively

> We *fought tooth and nail* to get that law overturned,
> and, after many months of hard work, we won.

bite (one's) tongue
to control (one's) emotion or speech

> I wanted to tell Lucy exactly what I thought of her
> bad behavior, but I *bit* my *tongue* and walked away.

lip service
a dishonest agreement

> She promised that those items would be delivered
> on time, but now I see that she was just giving me
> *lip service.*

keep (one's) chin up
to be courageous in the face of difficulty

> Life was hard for Jorge right after his wife died.
> But, he *kept* his *chin up* and is doing better.

stick (one's) neck out
to take a risk

> Are you sure you want to *stick* your *neck out* and
> tell the boss what you really think about this?

a pain in the neck / ass
an annoying thing or person

> Commuting is disagreeable most days, but in bad weather, it's *a real pain in the neck.*

chip on (one's) shoulder
to be always ready for any conflict

> Evan has had a rather terrible life. Maybe that's why he always seems to have a *chip on* his *shoulder.*

give (someone) the cold shoulder
to deliberately ignore

> Rex doesn't know why his friend Oleg *gave* him *the cold shoulder* when they saw each other at the concert last night.

an arm and a leg
an unreasonably high price

> Gosh, that sofa's beautiful, but it costs *an arm and a leg.* Too expensive for me!

twist (one's) arm
to force into action

> You're invited to the party, although no one is going to *twist* your *arm* to get you to come.

hand over fist
at a sizable rate or amount

[Since opening his dog grooming
business, Wes is making money
hand over fist.]

lend (someone) a hand
to assist (someone)

[Victor is painting his apartment this weekend and
we said we would *lend* him *a hand.*]

change hands
to pass from one owner to another

[This oil painting has *changed hands* several times,
but it has a permanent home with us now.]

old hand
someone with a great deal of experience

[If you raise sheep, you'll need to find a shearer.
Tom's an *old hand* at that, so you should call him.]

all thumbs
clumsy or awkward

[When she first learned to knit, Jocelyn was *all
thumbs*, but now she's an expert.]

keep (one's) fingers crossed
to hope nothing bad will happen

> I heard you're up for a promotion. Good luck! I'll
> *keep* my *fingers crossed* for you.

sticky fingers
to have a tendency to steal

> Ivy was shocked when she learned that her sister-
> in-law had *sticky fingers* and often took things
> from Ivy's home.

wrap (someone) around (one's) finger
to have complete control over (someone)

> Vivian has *wrapped* her husband *around* her *finger*
> and he'll do anything she says.

stab (someone) in the back
to do harm to (someone) without their knowledge

> Be careful what you tell Leah. She'll use it to *stab*
> you *in the back* if it suits her.

bust (one's) chops / balls
to deliberately tease or annoy (someone)

> Milo was kidding you. He told you he was dating
> your ex-girlfriend just to *bust* your *chops*.

on its last legs
on the brink of failing or dying

> Hank's fifteen-year-old car is *on its last legs* and he will have to buy another car soon.

pull (someone's) leg
to tease or trick (someone)

> I wasn't sure if Arianna was *pulling* my *leg* or not when she told me she was pregnant.

shake a leg
hurry

> You'd better *shake a leg* if you don't want to miss your bus.

a leg to stand on
having a good explanation, reason or excuse

> The thief was arrested for stealing jewelry. In court, he didn't have *a leg to stand on*, so he pled guilty.

get (one's) feet wet
to try something for the first time

> That new pottery store in town is offering classes. I'm thinking of *getting* my *feet wet* and trying a beginner's class.

cold feet
> *being too fearful to try or to complete an action*

>> Lily was going to try out for the band, but at the
>> last minute, she got *cold feet* and didn't audition.

best foot forward
> *a favorable first impression*

>> When you go to that job interview tomorrow,
>> make sure to put your *best foot forward.*

make no bones about it
> *to be completely honest*

>> You should tell him exactly what
>> you think about this problem and
>> *make no bones about it.*

bone up on
> *to study*

>> My certification exam is
>> next Tuesday. I have to
>> *bone up on* some of the
>> facts again before then.

get on (one's) nerves
> *to anger or annoy (someone)*

>> My co-worker whistles constantly while she works
>> and it really *gets on* my *nerves.*

get under (one's) skin
to disturb, upset or annoy very much

> Yes, Matthew's behavior is annoying, but don't let
> him *get under* your *skin.*

pull (one's) weight
to do (one's) fair share of the work

> Claudia was hired as a stylist at the hair salon two
> months ago and we are still waiting for her *to pull*
> her *weight.*

not on your life
never; not for any reason whatsoever

> "Would you ever go sky diving, Keira?"
> "*Not on your life.* I think it's too dangerous."

Every Body Idioms Exercise – Section 1:

1. Adina had a lot of work to finish by the end of the day and asked if I could _____ her _____ to get it all done.

2. My stapler disappeared yesterday and today my note pad is gone. Someone in this office has _____.

3. The copier machine in the office is _____ _____. We'll have to get a new one soon.

4. I'll have to _____ the latest statistics before I give that presentation on Monday.

5. Can we meet _____ to discuss this new project?

6. Kenzo didn't want to go out to dinner, but we _____ his _____ and made him come with us.

7. Because his new assistant was still _____ _____, the electrician had to rewire the house by himself.

8. Lionel got _____ and didn't propose marriage to his girlfriend Saturday night as he had planned.

9. That song is _____ my _____. Could you turn down the radio please?

10. The folder you've been looking for is _____ your _____.

11. Oh, we're late! We'll have to _____
    if we want to get to the movie on time.

12. Zeljko _____ for
    sole custody of his child.

13. Tibor and Ed have disagreed about this situation for a long
    time and will never _____ about it.

14. Let's _____ our _____ that
    our company gets that new contract and we keep our jobs.

15. What a good worker Joe is. He's here every day, _____
    _____, quietly doing his job.

16. Meg is _____ about the
    young man she met six months ago at your party.

17. We've been planning to redecorate our kitchen for a while
    now. I can't wait to _____ my _____
    it this weekend.

18. Why is Nick _____ me _____
    _____? Is he mad at me for something?

19. If no money _____, the car was
    a gift.

20. Carlo is used to ignoring his wife's endless complaints. They
    go _____.

21. Paulina gets anything she wants from her parents; she has
    them both _____ her _____.

22. When Taddeus met his girlfriend's parents for the first time, he _____ his _____ to impress them.

23. Simon is making money _____ at his new job on Wall Street.

24. Don't get your _____ just because I won't go with you to your mother's this weekend.

25. Did you really win the lottery or are you _____ my _____?

26. When he addressed the long-haired young man at the counter as "Miss," Giorgio _____ his _____ his _____.

27. I'm not sure what we're doing after the game on Saturday. Let's _____ then, ok?

28. Nell was very tempted to tell Andy what she thought of him, but she _____ her _____ and kept quiet.

Answer key begins on page 103

Every Body Idioms Exercise – Section 2:

29. Sal tries to fix things around the house, but he is _____.

30. You can't continue to _____ your son's bad behavior in school.

31. Serena thought Milly was her best friend until Milly _____ her _____ and stole her boyfriend.

32. I don't want anyone to know what we're planning, so _____ your _____ about it.

33. Oliver _____ for that gold watch. He could have bought it for much less at another store.

34. Watch this. I'm going to _____ Tom's _____ about his missing that shot in the game this afternoon.

35. Caleb is a great worker and _____ his _____ on every project.

36. If you _____ your _____, you can figure out how to save more money each month.

37. The meeting with my ex-husband's lawyer was very unpleasant and _____ my _____.

38. Whenever we go out to dinner, Al complains about everything. Why does he have to be such _____ _____?

39. Since getting out of jail, Devon has _____ his _____ _____ and is working hard at his job.

40. I'm not going to _____ my _____ and complain if the rest of you aren't going to do it with me.

41. Maggie's an _____ at real estate. She'll help you sell your house and find you a new one to buy.

42. I've never gone snowboarding, but I'm going to _____ my
    _____ and try it this weekend at that
    local resort.

43. You won't solve your problems unless you stop _____
    your _____ and face them.

44. Buy the sweater or not. It's _____
    my _____ either way!

45. If you're so upset with him, why don't you _____ Neal
    _____ your _____?

46. You may think you're right about this issue, but you don't
    have _____.

47. Raising children today is not easy, _____
    _____.

48. Stay away from that guy. He walks around with a _____
    _____ his _____ and is always looking for a fight.

49. The salesman kept insisting he would give me a good deal,
    but after awhile I realized it was just _____.

50. Because Lidia refused to help her brother settle their late
    mother's estate, getting her inheritance was delayed. Just
    another case of her _____ her _____
    _____ her _____.

51. Would I like to eat some scorpions? _____
    _____, thanks all the same.

52. The audience was _____ when the famous poet began to read from his latest book.

53. Did you see the ticket price on that Broadway show? It costs _____!

54. I know you don't like Martin, but don't let him _____ _____ your _____.

55. Things are tough at home now, but _____ your _____. Everything will get better soon.

Answer key begins on page 106

Get in on the Action

Now that you *know the ropes*, you should *get a kick out of* the next group of idioms.

a song and a dance
> *a complicated story meant to deceive or mislead*

> Why can't Tyson just tell you what happened last night instead of giving you *a song and a dance*?

go / come along for the ride
> *to accompany without playing an active part*

> We're going to the marina to check on the boat on Saturday. Want to *come along for the ride*?

a hop, skip, and a jump
> *a short distance*

> Ellen was so happy when her son and his family moved nearby. Now, her grandchildren are only *a hop, skip, and a jump* away and she can see them more often.

get a kick out of
  enjoy

> When she was young, Rei enjoyed skiing, but as she
> has grown older, she no longer *gets a kick out of* it.

sweep (something) under the rug
  to hide (something)

> Victor's bad gambling problem has put him deep in
> debt. *Sweeping* it *under the rug* will not help him.

jump the gun
  to begin doing something too soon

> This isn't the best time to sell your
> house, so don't *jump the gun* on such
> an important decision.

out of the running
  no longer in a competition

> Although Manus and I both applied for that job,
> he has already been called in for an interview.
> I guess I'm *out of the running*.

down to the wire
  to the every end, as in a race or contest

> It was hard to make a final decision about which
> person to hire. It came right *down to the wire*
> before we selected Christopher.

know the ropes
to be familiar with the details of something

> Shaun had been a short-order cook for more than ten years, so he *knew the ropes* when he began to work at our luncheonette.

hit below the belt
to say something that is very mean and cruel

> What Judy said to me was mean, but Allen's remark really *hit below the belt* and was very upsetting.

roll with the punches
to survive difficulties

> Pedro's life has been hard. Even so, he always *rolls with the punches* and never lets anything defeat him.

throw in the towel
to quit in defeat

> Adita had been applying for one job after the other for almost a year and was ready to *throw in the towel* when she was finally hired at that new company in town.

behind the eight ball
in an unfavorable position

> Jia found himself *behind the eight ball* when he lost
> his job and had to borrow money to pay his taxes.

on the ball
alert, capable and effective

> The teacher was pleased to see that her new aide
> seemed to be *on the ball* right from the start.

play ball
to co-operate

> You and Aaron may not like each other, but you
> have to *play ball* and work together on this job.

whole new ball game
an entirely different matter

> First you said you wanted to build a patio; now you
> want to put up a deck. That's a *whole new ball game*
> in terms of materials and cost, you know.

skate on thin ice
> *to be in a risky situation*

It's risky enough to borrow money to start a new business. If you use your savings to do it, you will be *skating on thin ice* financially.

sink or swim
> *to have the choice of only succeeding or failing*

Alfredo knew it was *sink or swim* when he started his T-shirt printing business last year. At any rate, he worked hard and soon made it a success.

smooth sailing
> *easy progress*

Now that Ramona has learned that new computer program, it's been *smooth sailing* for her to get her work done.

make waves
> *to cause a disturbance or a dispute*

> Everyone in our family gets along except for Tom.
> He's not happy unless he's *making waves* and upsetting someone else.

in the same boat
> *in a similar situation*

> Sarah was sorry when Nate lost his job, but then
> she lost hers too. Suddenly the two friends were *in
> the same boat.*

miss the boat
> *to fail to take advantage of an opportunity; to not understand*

> Too bad you didn't buy gold when it was $50.00
> an ounce. You really *missed the boat* on a great
> opportunity.

rock the boat
> *to upset the routine*

> You may not like it, but this is the way things are
> done at this company. It won't help to *rock the boat.*

run a tight ship
  to control in a strict, orderly way

> The new manager let everyone know immediately
> that he was going to *run a tight ship*: no coming in
> late, no leaving early, and no slacking on the job!

shape up or ship out
  behave or leave

> That new employee isn't performing very well.
> If he doesn't improve soon, he'll be told to *shape
> up or ship out.*

in the cards
  likely or certain to happen

> Ming isn't sure what's
> *in the cards* for him
> and his family next
> year, but he hopes
> things will be better.

put (one's) cards on the table
  to reveal clearly and honestly (one's) motives or intentions

> If we're going to negotiate this contract so that it
> is fair to everyone, we each need to *put* our *cards
> on the table* right from the start.

Get in on the Action Idioms Exercise

1. Lou is a good fair boss, but he _____ _____ and expects everyone to follow the rules.

2. Make those payments on your credit card or you will soon be _____ and owe even more money.

3. Please don't give me another _____ _____ about why you are late for work again today.

4. Those of us who are unemployed are _____ _____ when it comes to trying to put food on the table for our families.

5. Bill is pretty tough. No matter how bad things get at work or at home he always seems to _____ _____.

6. The judging at Saturday night's dance contest _____ _____. Paul and Tatiana managed to win by one vote.

7. I have no interest in deep sea fishing, but when my friends planned a trip, I decided to _____ _____ as it was a nice day to be out on the ocean.

8. Walt hid his illness for months, but it's impossible to _____ that kind of thing _____ for long.

9. I'm happy to know it's been _____ for them since they brought their new baby home from the hospital.

10. Writing books was one thing; promoting them in book stores and on TV was a _____ for the author.

11. Skye was disappointed to learn that she was _____ _____ for the grand prize in the quilting competition.

12. Before this problem can be settled, everyone has to _____ their _____ so we all know where we stand.

13. Kevin has bought many used cars, so he is a good person to take with you for advice as he _____.

14. That was rather mean of Angela to criticize your new hairdo. It's not like her to _____ like that.

15. Please don't _____ at Aunt Prita's birthday party by reminding her that she owes us money.

16. Yay! My favorite boutique just opened a new store _____ _____ away from my house!

17. Bonita is _____ at work as she never gets her work done on time.

18. There are only five waiters here tonight for dinner service, so they will all need to track their orders and to be _____ _____.

19. Louisa helps at the animal shelter as she _____ _____ walking the dogs and playing with the cats while they await adoption.

20. Told you to ask her out. Now Jim's dating her and you, my friend, have _____ again.

21. Who knows the future? I don't know what's _____ _____ for me next year and neither do you.

22. It was _____ time for the young company when, after months of preparation, it launched its first website.

23. This is the fifth time we've had to discipline you this year for poor work. For the last time, _____ _____.

24. You've worked so hard for your degree. Don't _____ _____ now that you're almost finished.

25. Let the buyer make an offer first. Don't _____ _____ and give him a price that might be lower than what he's willing to pay.

26. Peter loves to _____ at town hall meetings by asking challenging questions.

27. In order to get this sales contract, I will have to _____ _____ with Renaldo, whom I dislike intensely.

Answer key begins on page 108

Economics

Dollars to doughnuts, these are good idioms to *save for a rainy day*.

here goes nothing
> *with no expectations*

> I've never eaten Japanese food before, but this dish smells very good, so *here goes nothing*.

nothing doing
> *certainly not*

> Isabella asked me if I was inviting my ex-husband and his new wife to my cookout next weekend. I told her *nothing doing*.

nothing to it
> *to be very easy*

> We thought that hiking up that mountain would be hard, but, surprisingly, there was *nothing to it*.

stop at nothing
to do everything to achieve success

> Madeline will *stop at nothing* to win the annual cooking competition.

I owe (someone) one
A statement to say that you owe someone a kindness in return for their kindness to you.

> Thanks for shovelling the snow from my sidewalk while I was sick. *I owe* you *one.*

no two ways about it
no room for a different opinion or position

> Her parents decided that Claudia was still too young to go to a music concert and, *no two ways about it*, their decision was final.

put two and two together
to understand after learning all the facts

> At first, Valerie didn't understand why the manager at her bank always came out of his office to greet her. Then she *put two and two together* and realized it was because he liked her.

think twice
> *to consider carefully*

[I'd *think twice* before agreeing to drive across the
country with a complete stranger.]

six of one, half dozen of another
> *to be equal*

[If both stores are selling those floor tiles for the
same price, it doesn't matter where we buy them,
right? I mean, *six of one, half dozen of another.*]

catch-22
> *a situation where the right outcome is impossible because of
> illogical rules or conditions*

[The problem for young people entering the work
force is always the same: they need a job to get
experience but they often need experience to get a
job. It's a real *catch-22* for them.]

a pretty penny
> *a high price*

[Completely renovating that old house is going to
cost the young owners *a pretty penny.*]

pinch pennies
to economize

> Last month, Mathis stopped buying
> coffee on his way to work in an effort
> to *pinch pennies*.

put in (one's) two cents
to give (one's) opinion

> Please don't talk about our financial problems in
> front of your mother. I'd rather she not *put in* her
> *two cents* on this subject.

a dime a dozen
commonplace and overly abundant

> Vampires are in so many TV shows and movies;
> they've become *a dime a dozen*. How about a new
> monster for a change?

dollars to doughnuts
a sure thing; a certainty

> Anyone can see that those two are very much in
> love. *Dollars to doughnuts* they get married within
> the year.

fast buck
> *money earned quickly and easily*

> Pam told Ed he could earn a
> *fast buck* if he would bring his
> van to her aunt's house on
> Saturday and help her move.

pass the buck
> *to shift blame from (one) to (another)*

> Geraldo makes mistakes at work, then *passes the
> buck,* blaming everyone else for his errors.

rags to riches
> *from extreme poverty to wealth*

> When that homeless man won the lottery, he went
> from *rags to riches* overnight.

save for a rainy day
> *to save for any future difficulties*

> Hatsue was taught to *save for a rainy day* and now
> has a great deal of money in her bank account.

Economic Idioms Exercise

1. That's a beautiful leather coat. I'll bet it cost you _____
    _____.

2. Thanks for picking me up when my car broke down today.
    _____.

3. Karl asked us to lend him a thousand dollars, but since he
    never repaid his last loan, we told him _____
    _____.

4. Want to make a _____? Deliver these
    printed samples to the City and I'll pay you $25 cash when
    you get back.

5. Her mom's all-time favorite singer was Nat King Cole, _____
    _____.

6. You can easily find those plain window blinds in any hard-
    ware store. They're _____
    and nothing special.

7. Don't be afraid to go snorkeling. It's easy. Believe me, there's
    _____.

8. Sanjay's becoming a millionaire after such humble begin-
    nings is a very inspiring _____
    story.

9. I don't know which house painter we should hire. They're
    both professional and not too expensive, so _____
    _____, pick either one.

10. Glad to see you finally _____
_____ and figured out that Sammo is not your friend.

11. Come on, I'll treat you to lunch. I know you've been _____
_____ lately.

12. Paying the cable bill was your responsibility and you forgot.
Don't _____ and blame it on me.

13. Eric has to take a Japanese literature class in order to get his
degree, but his college no longer offers that course. What a
_____.

14. Sergio will _____ to get
Sophia to marry him.

15. Lex is a good friend. He knows how to listen, but doesn't
_____ his _____ unless I ask
him for his advice.

16. Susan and James always intended to _____
_____, but somehow they never did.

17. Luis is working too hard lately. _____
_____ it's going to catch up to him very soon.

18. I'm asking you to _____ before
contributing any money to his cause.

19. Antonio has never directed a movie before? Oh great! _____
_____.

Answer key begins on page 110

Worldly Goods

Learning this next set of idioms won't have you *over a barrel*.

pass the hat
   to take up a collection of money

> We're *passing the hat* for Maya's going away party on Friday. Can you throw in a few bucks?

talk through (one's) hat
   to say things that are incorrect or unproven

> Ravi told you he's buying a Ferrari? You can't believe anything he says, you know. He's always *talking through* his *hat*.

wear many / several hats
   to do several jobs or several parts of a job

> As the owner and publisher of the local newspaper, Yves *wears several hats*: he's the reporter, editor, photographer, layout artist, and printer.

under (one's) hat
to keep secret or private

> Claudia gave him the information and warned
> him to keep it *under* his *hat* until Friday.

keep (one's) shirt on
to remain calm or patient

> I'm getting this done as fast as I can, so please *keep*
> your *shirt on* and give me another minute.

lose (one's) shirt
to lose everything (one) has

> Brandon put every cent he had into a video rental
> business and *lost* his *shirt* after only five years.

hot under the collar
to be angry

> At dinner last night, Karen's husband got a little
> *hot under the collar* when he thought the waiter
> was flirting with her.

rob the cradle
to date or marry someone much younger than oneself

> Jenna's parents are not happy that her fiance is 30
> years older than she, and they didn't hesitate to tell
> her that he's *robbing the cradle*.

get up on the wrong side of the bed
to act unpleasantly due to a bad start to the day

> Peter's so grumpy today. He must have *gotten up on the wrong side of the bed* this morning.

off (one's) rocker
crazy

> Olivia must be *off* her *rocker* if she thinks we can still be friends after the horrible things she said about me.

under the table
secretly

> Ted prefers to hire high school kids to work part time in his deli and to pay them *under the table*.

turn the tables
to gain an advantage by reversing a situation

> Adish was losing his chess game when he suddenly saw how to *turn the tables* on his opponent and win.

put through the wringer
to go through a serious experience

> Poor Natasha. First, her husband was very ill for several months, then she got sick as well. She was *put through the wringer* last year.

no soap / no dice / no go
certainly not

> When Diane asked her older brother to tell their parents about her bad report card, he said, "*No soap.* Do it yourself."

burn the candle at both ends
work or play too hard without resting

> Joel has been studying every weeknight and partying every weekend. He's going to be in trouble soon if he keeps *burning the candle at both ends.*

a drop in the bucket
an insufficient amount compared to what is needed

> Miguel's contribution is greatly appreciated, though it is only *a drop in the bucket* compared to the total amount needed.

lock, stock and barrel
the whole of anything, including every piece

> They bought a dry cleaning business in town, *lock, stock and barrel,* and are doing very well running it.

get the ax
get or be fired from a job

> Did you hear about Bruce? He got
> to the office on Monday morning
> and immediately *got the ax.*

hit the hay / sack
go to bed

> Gosh, I'm really tired. I'm going to *hit the hay* early
> tonight.

hit the nail on the head
*to make a correct guess or analysis; to say or do exactly what's
right*

> David *hit the nail on the head* when he guessed
> that redecorating the bathroom would cost about
> $2,000.

hit the roof
to be very angry

> Glenn *hit the roof* when his wife told him that
> she had donated his old golf clubs to the church
> rummage sale.

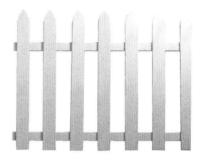

on the fence
undecided as to which of two sides to support

> Vanessa hasn't decided how she is going to vote in the upcoming election. She is still *on the fence* as to which candidate to support.

on the wagon
avoiding alcoholic beverages

> Charles stopped drinking alcohol several years ago and has been *on the wagon* ever since.

over a barrel
in a helpless or awkward position; unable to act in one's own interests

> When Theresa saw Ann cheating on a test, she threatened to report her unless Ann gave her the baby blue cashmere sweater she was wearing. Ann is *over a barrel* as she doesn't want to admit to cheating nor does she want to give Theresa her new cashmere sweater.

Worldly Goods Idioms Exercise

1. Ray's going to walk barefoot across the entire country. He's not _____ though; he's raising money for charity.

2. Considering that you owe her a thousand dollars, giving her ten dollars is barely _____.

3. Gloria _____ when she guessed that Reggie would propose to Emily on her birthday.

4. I'll share my secret with you if you promise to keep it _____ your _____ until I tell you otherwise.

5. If Alexandra is late for work one more time, she's going to _____.

6. I'm still _____ about whether to paint the bedroom dark gray or a pale blue.

7. He'll pay you _____ if you help him remove that junk from the school basement.

8. I'm having such a terrible day. I feel like I _____ _____ this morning.

9. Beth asked if she could drive my new Mercedes to Reno and I told her, "_____."

10. Theo just learned that his young daughter needs another expensive operation. Let's _____ for him this week.

11. The sellers thought they had each of us _____ _____ because we were both interested in buying their house. But I found another house that I liked better and bought that one.

12. Don't get so _____, pal. No one is bothering your girlfriend.

13. Please call me before nine tonight. I'm planning to _____ _____ early and get a good night's sleep.

14. Pam's friends were shocked that she was dating someone ten years younger; however, Pam evidently doesn't mind _____ _____.

15. You can't believe what Marita might tell you about her experiences working in Hollywood. She has a tendency to _____ her _____.

16. That company had me fill out tons of forms, take several tests, and generally _____ me _____ _____. Then they didn't hire me!

17. Iris decided to go _____ for a few months in an effort to lose more weight.

18. You'd better slow down. You've been _____ _____ for the past six months, and you're going to regret it soon, trust me.

19. They bought the house as well as everything in it, _____ _____.

20. The deal they offered you is not very good. In my opinion, if you put your money into it, you'll _____ your _____.

21. Lester _____ when the final bill for his son's dental work came in yesterday's mail.

22. Rachel was about to tell John that she didn't want to date him any longer when he _____ on her and told her the same thing.

23. Relax man! We're almost there. _____ your _____ _____!

24. When he worked in the movie theater, Diego _____ _____: he sold the tickets, ran the snack concession, showed the movies, and cleaned up the theater every night.

Answer key begins on page 112

It's Only Natural

Learning these idioms will be *a walk in the park.*

day in and day out
> *every day without fail; continuously*

> Moira has been working on her painting *day in and day out* in order to finish it in time for next month's exhibition.

in hot water
> *in a great amount of trouble*

> Shona's father told her that she'd be *in hot water* if she came home late again that night.

break the ice
> *to make a start; to relax a tense social situation*

> Everyone at the meeting was very nervous as we expected bad news. Then the boss *broke the ice* with a joke and assured us that the news was good.

full of hot air
excessive and exaggerated talking

> Whew! The man who sat next to me on
> the train this morning was so *full of hot
> air*. I couldn't wait to get away from him.

fight fire with fire
to react to something in the same manner

> If James is going to bring up my past problems
> with alcohol, I'm going to *fight fire with fire* and
> remind him of his past drug abuse.

a walk in the park
easy

> Getting to and from the airport to pick up Uncle
> Josef was *a walk in the park* — this time.

beat around the bush
to avoid dealing with the important part of something

> Alma certainly didn't *beat around the bush* when
> she told Frank exactly why he was being fired.

out of the woods
out of danger

> Keshia was ill for several months, but she is finally
> *out of the woods* and on her way to a full recovery.

between a rock and a hard place
between two equally bad choices

> Loretta doesn't want to take that job as a waitress
> with its low pay and long hours, but she owes two
> months' rent and has no other job offers. She's
> caught *between a rock and a hard place.*

turn over a new leaf
to change for the better

> Calvin was in a gang when he was a teenager and
> got into a lot of trouble. Now that he is a young
> father, he has *turned over a new leaf* and is living a
> much better life.

no bed of roses
to not be in a comfortable position or situation

> Dealing with my mom's doctors and attorneys, as
> well as with my two brothers, was *no bed of roses,*
> but someone had to step in and take care of things
> during her final illness.

sleep like a log
to sleep very deeply

> Irina was so tired after running
> in the 15K marathon yesterday
> that she *slept like a log* last night.

under the weather
feeling unwell

> Victor has been *under the weather* lately and hasn't
> been his usual cheerful self at work.

high and dry
in a helpless position

> Greg promised to pick me up at the dentist's office,
> but he forgot and left me *high and dry* with no way
> to get home.

run hot and cold
to be inconsistent

> Amy *runs hot and cold* when it comes to her career.
> One day she says she wants more responsibilities
> and the next, she doesn't.

the last straw
the event that finally goes beyond what (one) can accept

> When the plumber cancelled his appointment for
> the sixth time, it was *the last straw* and we hired
> someone else.

It's Only Natural Idioms Exercise

1. Tell me exactly what's on your mind and don't _____
   _____.

2. We won't go to the mall on Saturday if you're still feeling
   _____.

3. When the company suddenly closed, its 90 employees were
   left _____ with no income
   and no health insurance.

4. Running a dog grooming salon was _____
   _____ for Kendra compared to working at
   the veterinarian's office.

5. Variel _____ when it
   comes to José; one day she is in love with him and the next
   day, she isn't.

6. Adam's parents remained at the hospital after their infant
   son's surgery until he was completely _____
   _____.

7. Clark has been working _____
   _____ to find new homes for the orphaned children.

8. Dennis _____ last night
   after biking 25 miles yesterday afternoon.

9. Do you think that when Francine gets out of jail she will ____
   _____ and lead a better life?

10. When Will and Robin decided to divorce, they _____
_____ to get what each wanted in the
final judgment.

11. Go ahead. Offer to buy that woman a drink just to _____
_____ and see if she'll talk to you.

12. Eva's comment about my crooked teeth was _____
_____. I'm not going to forgive her for her
insults anymore.

13. Some choice. Hector can start working the overnight shift at
the factory next month or keep working days and take a 15%
pay cut. He's caught _____
_____.

14. That Cosmo is _____.
It's not possible that he went lion hunting in Africa last week.

15. I'll be _____ with my
parents if I don't get at least a C in math this semester.

16. Working with both the workers' union and management was
_____ but a
new contract was finally agreed upon.

Answer key begins on page 115

Rainbow

Students have *the green light* to continue with this colorful group of idioms.

in the pink
> *healthy*

>> Michelle has been feeling *in the pink* since she started her new diet and exercise program.

in the red
> *in debt*

>> Right now we are *in the red* and we need to start earning more money soon.

paint the town red
> *to go out and have a good time*

>> When Earl and Carol won the sweepstakes, they went out that weekend and *painted the town red*.

red tape
bureaucratic procedures that delay progress

> After six months of *red tape*, the young couple was able to bring their adopted daughter home.

see red
to become very angry

> Every time Deanna thinks about how she was cheated out of her money, she *sees red*.

catch (someone) red-handed
to catch (someone) in the act of doing something wrong

> When Ernest went to his office late last night, he *caught* his partner *red-handed* stealing money from the safe.

out of the blue
suddenly

> The phone call from her old school friend came *out of the blue* last Tuesday.

once in a blue moon
only rarely over a long period of time

> We used to go out to eat at least once a week. Now we can only afford to eat out *once in a blue moon*.

blue in the face
to the greatest possible point

His mother pleaded with him until she was *blue in the face*, but Cyril refused to get a job.

the green light
permission to go ahead with something

You've got *the green light* to handle this project. Make sure you do a good job.

green around the gills
to look sick

After he ate the mussels, Gabe looked a little *green around the gills* and quickly left the restaurant.

black mark
a mark of failure

I'm afraid that this mistake will be a *black mark* against you.

the pot calling the kettle black
criticizing others for the faults (one) also has

For someone with 200 pairs of shoes, Imelda has no right to criticize her sister for buying yet another handbag. That's *the pot calling the kettle black*, isn't it?

gray matter
> *brains or intelligence*

> If you would use a little more of your *gray matter,*
> you would be able to solve this problem easily.

a gold mine
> *a great source of wealth*

> Buying that corner luncheonette proved to be *a*
> *gold mine* for the talented young chef.

Rainbow Idioms Exercise

1. They've only been dating for a month, so Marco's marriage proposal to Leann came _____.

2. Frank's work habits are so poor, he must have several _____ _____ against him.

3. Is Gareth getting ill? He looks a bit _____ _____.

4. They've been _____ for many months, but with Tao's new job, they can start paying down their debts.

5. Emil needs to be challenged to use more of his _____ _____ so he can improve as a student.

6. You can tell her to save money until you are _____ _____. If she doesn't want to do it, she won't.

7. C'mon. I'm tired of staying home all the time. Let's go out tonight and _____ for a change.

8. He thought that owning a car wash would be _____ _____, but it didn't earn as much money as he had hoped.

9. We are just waiting to get _____ from you so we can start renovating your kitchen.

10. Nardo gambled away all his money and is bankrupt. For him to criticize his brother for playing poker with his friends is _____.

11. We had to wade through a ton of _____ before we could get the business registered in the state's vendor database.

12. They were happy to hear that Melissa is back _____ _____ after her bicycle accident.

13. Generally, they don't eat fast food, but, _____ _____ they'll stop for a hamburger and some fries.

14. No one knew who was vandalizing the classrooms until Mrs. Brown _____ a student _____.

15. Every time Yasuo talks about his first wife, his second wife _____.

Answer key begins on page 116

Grab Bag

Don't *call it quits* yet. *Believe it or not*, you're still *on the right track* with this last group of idioms.

all work and no play
: *hard work with no time for fun*

> You've been working for months on your term paper; it's been *all work and no play* for you. How about we go out for dinner tonight?

believe it or not
: *true, even if (one) doesn't believe it*

> Hey, *believe it or not*, Jackie got promoted to the Unit Manager position over Sam.

bend over backwards
: *to be very forgiving, understanding, or patient*

> Irma *bends over backwards* for her youngest sister whenever Agnes needs help with something.

bite off more than (one) can chew
to attempt something beyond (one's) abilities

> When Norm decided to repaper
> his kitchen, he had never put up
> wallpaper before. Once he started,
> he realized he had *bitten off more*
> *than* he *could chew.*

bite the bullet
to adjust to unpleasant circumstances

> Money is scarce right now so we're going to have
> to *bite the bullet* and stop spending so much.

the blind leading the blind
when leaders know as little as their followers

> No one in that government office seems to know
> who's in charge or what he or she is doing. It's like
> *the blind leading the blind* in there.

change (one's) tune
to reverse (one's) views or opinions

> Pei Zi had nothing good to say about that depart-
> ment until she was offered a job there. She *changed*
> her *tune* about it quickly after that.

call it a day
> *to stop an activity for the remainder of the day*

> Thank you all for your hard work today. Let's *call it a day* and start again tomorrow.

call it quits
> *to end an activity or effort*

> They've been struggling to make their marriage work, but last week, Clint and Judy finally decided to *call it quits*.

call the shots
> *to have the power to make decisions*

> The printer needs someone to give him the final quantity on these brochures. Who is *calling the shots* on this project?

a cheap shot
> *a deliberately unfair attack, usually with words*

> Margo's unkind remark about her brother's weight was rather *a cheap shot*.

cut down on
> *to use less of something*

> The doctor told his overweight patient to *cut down on* her salt and fat consumption.

do the trick
to achieve a good result

> If you just tighten this screw right here, that should *do the trick*.

down the drain
wasted or lost; gone

> That company went bankrupt and the investors' money went *down the drain*.

draw the line
to set a limit, as for acceptable behavior

> I'll help them find a lawyer, but I *draw the line* at helping them pay for one.

easy come, easy go
a lack of concern over something that (one) gets and loses, especially money

> Leo won $200 in the football pool at work Monday. That night his water heater broke and it will cost $200 to fix! Oh well, *easy come, easy go*.

face the music
to accept the unpleasant results of (one's) own actions

> Your son has gotten away with some mischief in the past. Now, he will have to *face the music* for the serious damage he has caused.

fair and square
honest and just

> Kaz is a good plumber; he does good work and his prices are *fair and square.*

fair shake
honest treatment

> Everyone likes to work for that supervisor as he gives all his employees a *fair shake.*

fat chance
little or no chance

> Ian really thinks he's going to win that election over me? *Fat chance!*

get to the bottom of (something)
to learn the real cause of (something)

> No one is going home until we *get to the bottom of* what's causing this software problem.

from the get-go
from the beginning

> Olaf's co-workers didn't like him *from the get-go.*
> Still, they have to work with him every day.

give (someone) a hard time
to annoy or make trouble for (someone)

> Marian hasn't done anything to you. Why are you
> *giving* her *a hard time*?

give it (one's) best shot
to try very hard

> We know you've never had this much responsibil-
> ity before, but we know you'll *give it* your *best shot.*

go from bad to worse
to get progressively worse

> The working conditions at Roberto's job weren't
> good to begin with, and recently they *went from*
> *bad to worse.*

by hook or by crook
by whatever means possible, whether fair or unfair

> Mark is determined to get a starring role in that
> Broadway play *by hook or by crook.*

in luck
> *fortunate*

>> Oh good, I'm *in luck*. That sweater I wanted to buy a month ago is on sale now.

in the long run
> *in the end*

>> You should prepare the walls before you paint them. *In the long run* it will make the job go faster.

in the nick of time
> *at the very last, but right moment*

>> We thought we might be late for the performance, but we got there *in the nick of time* and were seated just as the curtain rose.

Johnny-come-lately
> *one who arrives late and tries to make unwanted changes*

>> We had to deal with this problem for over a month and it's finally resolved. Why would we listen to his *Johnny-come-lately* ideas now?

keep tabs on
> *to watch carefully*

>> Our new supervisor is *keeping tabs on* everything so we need to get to work on time every day.

keep up with the Joneses
to try to get as many material goods as those around (one)

> Doug is so obsessed with *keeping up with the Joneses* that he doesn't enjoy what he already has.

lay down the law
to state with certainty

> As parents, Bob and Sonya definitely *lay down the law* for their four children.

leave well enough alone
to leave unchanged something that would be made worse if changed

> Greg's landscaping business was doing great until he stopped accepting small projects. Now business is slow. He should have *left well enough alone.*

too little, too late
limited help and not in time to be effective

> Karen's mother offered to lend her some money, but it was *too little, too late* and Karen's car was repossessed.

live and learn
> *to profit from experience*

>> We didn't enjoy our stay at that fancy resort at all.
>> *Live and learn*; we certainly won't go there again.

live it up
> *to enjoy oneself*

>> He's been working so hard lately that you can't
>> blame him if he wants to *live it up* this weekend.

lose sight of
> *to fail to account for*

>> Don't *lose sight of* the many reasons you chose to
>> become a dental assistant.

lose sleep over
> *to worry about (often used negatively:* don't *lose sleep over)*

>> There's nothing you can do to help your brother
>> with his problems, so don't *lose sleep over* it.

make ends meet
> *to live within (one's) means*

>> After they both lost their jobs last year, Jake and his
>> wife struggled to *make ends meet*.

miss the point
to not understand the important part of something

> The official *missed the point* of what the woman was telling him about a problem in the first section of the application form.

more (of something) than (one) can shake a stick at
a great amount, uncountable

> When Enrique knocked the hornet's nest from the tree, he was suddenly attacked by *more* angry hornets *than he could shake a stick at.*

no hard feelings
no anger or resentment

> Thanks for being such a good competitor. Now that I've won, I hope there will be *no hard feelings* between us.

no ifs, ands, or buts
no excuses

> You are expected to complete this assignment in two weeks, *no ifs, ands, or buts.*

no kidding
honestly; really

> They're moving to Melbourne, Australia next month? *No kidding?*

no picnic
not pleasant, difficult

> Moving a household of eight
> kids, five dogs, and a horse
> from California to Virginia
> was *no picnic* for that family.

no questions asked
with no additional information given

> Akiko couldn't believe the store took back the
> clothes she had purchased, *no questions asked.*

no sooner said than done
accomplished immediately

> Leslie asked her husband if they could get a new
> dishwasher and, *no sooner said than done*, they
> bought one and had it installed.

no way
under no conditions

> There is *no way* that Miranda's parents would ever
> let her move back into their home.

not know where to turn
to be confused about where or how to get help

> Steve didn't know whether to
> accept the new opening at
> work or not, and did*n't know*
> *where to turn* for advice.

not sleep a wink
to not sleep at all

> Bryan has been so worried about his son's poor
> health that he has*n't slept a wink* in many weeks.

off the hook
free from blame or obligation

> Joanna is going to head the renovation committee
> so you are *off the hook*.

on a roll
to have continued good luck

> Winston was *on a roll* last year: he got a great new
> job, met his fiancé, and inherited a house.

on the level
honest, without deception

> Let's go back to the first car dealer. The salesman
> there seemed to be more *on the level* than the one
> we just spoke to.

on the right track
following the correct set of plans or beliefs

> We're glad to see that Nando is *on the right track* at school after the trouble he got into last year.

on the same wavelength
to have similar thoughts or feelings

> We're such good friends because we always seem to be *on the same wavelength*.

out from under
no longer in a difficult position, as to be free from debt or obligations

> Now that Dan is earning more money, he and his wife are getting *out from under* many of their bills.

out of order
not operating properly or at all; not according to the rules

> That vending machine is *out of order*, but this one is working fine.

> The teacher gave the students a list that was *out of order* and told them to arrange it alphabetically.

out of the question
not possible

> The fourteen-year-old girl's parents told her it was *out of the question* for her to go camping alone.

out of touch
no longer in contact with

> Since graduation last year, Minoru has fallen *out of touch* with his college buddies.

play / act dumb
to pretend to not know something

> Even though the thief was caught with the stolen goods, he *played dumb* at the police station.

put up or shut up
offer to change something or continue to endure it

> Stefan complains about the way his wife handles their finances, but if he doesn't like it, he should *put up or shut up*.

quit while (one) is ahead
to stop doing something while that activity is going well

> Harvey had already won $1,000 in the poker game when he bet it all on his last hand and lost. He should have *quit while he was ahead*.

read between the lines
to understand the unstated but suggested meaning of something said or written

> Although Joaõ insisted there nothing was wrong, Katia could *read between the lines* and knew that something bad had happened.

rub it in
to stress something unpleasant in order to be annoying

> I feel bad enough that I didn't win. You don't have to *rub it in* too, do you?

rub (someone) the wrong way
to irritate or annoy (someone)

> Keep that new temp worker away from me, please! Something about her *rubs* me *the wrong way.*

short and sweet
pleasantly brief and appropriate

> When the actor got up to accept his award, he kept his speech *short and sweet.*

sick and tired
very weary

> Jürgen is *sick and tired* of his sister's constant whining about her job.

sit tight
to take no action

> As the economy is uncertain right now, we were
> advised to *sit tight* on some of our investments.

take sides
to support one opinion or position in a dispute

> Don't put me in the middle of your squabble. I like
> you both and won't *take sides*.

a tall order
a very difficult task or demand

> Otto is afraid of heights, so asking him to climb
> even a short stepladder is *a tall order* for him.

through thick and thin
to continue through good times and bad

> Mick and Donal have been best friends since
> childhood and have been *through thick and thin*
> together.

too good to be true
so good as to be unbelievable

> I thought his offer to rebuild our deck for $500 was
> *too good to be true* and I was right.

Grab Bag Idioms Exercise – Section 1

1. Paul completely _____ of what the doctor was telling him about his chemotherapy treatments.

2. You'll be better off _____ if you try to save some money each month.

3. Lynn's boss _____ to help her when she was having health problems.

4. The three friends got some unexpected cash and decided to go to Las Vegas and _____.

5. Boyd has _____ his alcohol consumption since he became ill.

6. Those two have been working together for so many years that they are _____.

7. Ray disliked his daughter's boyfriend right _____ _____.

8. When Jun Fai volunteered to head the committee, Shannon was glad she was _____ and wouldn't have to do it.

9. The paper arrived _____ and we were able to print the presentation notes before the meeting started.

10. Masha was delighted to hear from her cousin Pavel as they had been _____ for years.

11. He sold his stamp collection, went to a casino, and, _____ _____, lost all the money at the blackjack table.

12. Everyone in this group was working well together until the boss told us to include Dan. Why couldn't she _____ _____?

13. If you have teenage children, it's a good idea to _____ _____ where they are going and whom they are seeing.

14. Don't worry if you don't do it right the first time. Just _____ _____ your _____ and that will be fine.

15. Zach ran out of his cold medicine late last night. He was ____ _____ though, as the pharmacy is open 24 hours and he was able to get more.

16. All their plans to move to Costa Rico went _____ _____ when they lost all their money.

17. Oh no, this list of names is _____ and now I have to retype the whole thing.

18. Walter was _____ of his boring life and longed for some excitement.

19. We've been painting since early this morning and I'm exhausted. Let's _____ and have some dinner.

20. Anita puts so much effort into trying to _____ _____ even though she already has plenty.

21. The people next door had a very loud party last night and we did_____.

22. Fred's been avoiding speaking with his elderly parents about their finances, but he has to _____ and do it soon.

23. I'm sorry about arguing with you at work last week. I hope there are _____.

Answer key begins on page 117

Grab Bag Idioms Exercise – Section 2

24. The store didn't have the exact color thread I wanted so I bought something close that should _____.

25. You can _____, but everyone knows you were involved in getting Dennis fired.

26. The principal called the three students into her office to ____ _____ their constant fighting.

27. Gregory has agreed not to notify the police if his missing money is returned by tomorrow, _____.

28. Silvain often bragged about being a great goalie. He certainly _____ his _____ last night after his team lost the game.

29. What is Bianca going to do to _____ until she can get another job?

30. The company claimed there would be no layoffs next month. The workers _____ and suspected otherwise.

31. Passing the tests to get into graduate school was _____ _____, but Lorenzo was glad he had done it.

32. That real estate agent is _____ this month. She has sold two houses and listed three more.

33. As everyone is very busy today, I'll make this announcement _____ so we can all get right back to work.

34. Several students were suspected of inciting the riots, but it was hard to determine which one was _____ _____.

35. Melinda has been avoiding seeing a doctor about the mole on her back. She needs to _____ and make an appointment right away.

36. We're very busy, but please _____ and someone will help you in a moment.

37. I absolutely have to complete this project by next Tuesday, _____.

38. Since getting a pay raise, Ti Hua has been able to get _____ _____ most of his bills.

39. Luther's sculpture has to be finished in time for an exhibit in two months. The next several weeks will be _____ _____ for him.

40. Does Halle really expect to get an invitation to the royal wedding? _____!

41. Tanya loves to buy clothes. This past month alone she has bought _____ sweaters _____ you _____
    _____.

42. Neither the president nor the cabinet seems to know what to do in this crisis. It's like _____
    _____ in our government right now.

43. Rudy is tired of worrying about his sister's marital problems and is not going to _____ them any more.

44. Mr. and Mrs. Roth's bagel store was doing very well until they doubled its size. Now sales are the same but their costs are greater. They should have _____ they
    _____.

45. Emilio always offers to help his friends, but it's usually _____
    _____ because he's not really sincere.

46. Martin volunteered to lead this investigation, but he has
    _____ he _____
    and is struggling with his duties.

Answer key begins on page 120

Grab Bag Idioms Exercise – Section 3
This next section uses *two* idioms in each sentence.

47. Wasn't losing that race in front of her friends enough of a disappointment for Laura? Do you have to _____
    with _____ too?

48. Don't expect a _____ if Charles is your opponent. He is determined to win _____ _____.

49. I hate it when Veronica and Kazuko argue. I _____ _____ at _____ when it comes to my friends.

50. Georgia's financial situation has _____ _____. She can't pay her bills this month and does_____ for help.

51. Last year, Natasha's son kept getting into trouble in school. She _____ with him and now he is _____.

52. Kiho thought the seller was _____ but he should have known the price on that condo was _____ _____.

53. This morning, Shirley said that the copy machine was _____ _____ and _____ _____, it was repaired.

54. Although he had only one more year of studies to complete for his degree, Luke _____ why he wanted to be an engineer and decided to _____.

55. "_____, Jorge won the mega jackpot lottery twice in one year." "_____!"

56. Getting all this work done before Friday is _____, but it's not _____.

57. Those two friends have been _____
together and have always been _____
with each other.

58. Sharon has never liked Will. Something about him _____
her _____ and there's _____
she'd ever agree to work with him again.

59. Hey! Mr. _____! You criticize
everything we do after it's done. Why don't you _____
_____?

59. Hiring an assistant sounded like a good idea to Ross, but his
new employee has begun _____ him _____
about the long hours she is expected to work. _____
_____, right?

Answer key begins on page 122

Answer key for Chow Down Idioms Exercise

1. Ken works six days a week to <u>bring home the bacon</u> for his wife and four children.

2. Your <u>goose is cooked</u> if you're not home from work before 10 o'clock tonight.

3. Painting the bedroom walls was <u>a piece of cake / as easy as pie</u> and we finished sooner than we had expected.

4. When she walked into the classroom as a teacher for the first time, Linda felt <u>like a fish out of water</u>.

5. The boss <u>laid an egg</u> when he forgot to introduce the company president at the meeting.

6. Until he was injured, Rick had been earning his <u>bread and butter</u> as a roofer.

7. Carla gave up gambling <u>cold turkey</u> last year.

8. Did you <u>spill the beans</u> to her about our plans for tomorrow?

9. That business opportunity sounds risky. Maybe you shouldn't <u>put all</u> your <u>eggs in one basket</u>.

10. There are too many things to review right now. Let's just go over the <u>meat and potatoes</u> parts.

11. Do you think Sandra will ever become a doctor or is that just <u>pie in the sky</u>?

12. Okay, so you didn't win this beauty pageant. Don't <u>cry over spilled milk</u>; start preparing for the next competition.

13. You have such a terrible frown on your face today. <u>What's eating</u> you?

14. Desmond was nervous about having to make that important speech. When the time came, however, he was <u>as cool as a cucumber</u> and did a great job.

15. The car salesmen told you the car only had one owner, but I would <u>take</u> what he said <u>with a grain of salt</u>.

16. Maria has gone from being in one bad relationship to another. She keeps jumping <u>out of the frying pan and into the fire</u>.

17. Auditioning for a stage play can be nerve-wracking, but you're very talented, so don't <u>chicken out</u>.

18. Some movie stars want fame *and* privacy, but they can't <u>have</u> their <u>cake and eat it too</u>.

19. This job will require you to do many different things, <u>from soup to nuts</u>, every day.

20. The town council has decided not to extend our contract. <u>How do you like them / those apples</u>?

21. Sharif forgot to bring the file with his presentation on it and <u>had egg on</u> his <u>face</u> at the meeting.

22. As he picked his way across the fields, the lone soldier was a <u>sitting duck</u> for attack.

23. The landscaper bid on two jobs, but only got one. Sometimes in business <u>that's the way the cookie crumbles</u>.

24. I can't believe Joel asked for a raise as he is such a poor worker. That guy really <u>takes the cake</u>.

25. Kim was offered the job, but she turned it down because the pay was <u>chicken feed</u>.

26. I'll be happy to give you a ride to work next week. And you don't have to <u>butter</u> me <u>up</u> to get me to do it.

27. Here's some <u>food for thought</u>: how different would your life be if you were rich?

Answer key for Critters Exercise

1. This party was supposed to be a surprise, but someone <u>let the cat out of the bag</u> and spoiled it.

2. Nino won the lottery and, to celebrate, is <u>going whole hog</u> with a big party this weekend.

3. Wilfredo's wife hasn't been feeling well, so he has been <u>as quiet as a mouse</u> around the house.

4. It's easier to enjoy the <u>dog days</u> of summer if you live by a beach or lake and can go swimming to cool off.

5. Tom is such <u>a bull in a china shop</u> that his wife won't let him near her antique doll collection.

6. This new computer program may have cost a lot of money, but I've used it and I think it's <u>for the birds</u>.

7. If you don't do something romantic for your wife for Valentine's Day, you will definitely be <u>in the doghouse</u>.

8. Max says he will quit smoking but only <u>when pigs fly</u>.

9. When the lawyer asked the witness to state what she had seen, <u>the cat got</u> her <u>tongue</u> and she was silent.

10. Whenever Julie is at someone's house for dinner, she <u>eats like a bird</u> in an effort to be polite.

11. Although she <u>put the cart before the horse</u> and raised a family before going to college, Pam's new career is going well.

12. The boss will be away next week and it's up to you to see that there's no <u>monkey business</u> while he's gone.

13. Henry was in sales for many years but got tired of the <u>dog-eat-dog</u> environment.

14. Tell the crowd at the door to <u>hold</u> their <u>horses</u>; they'll be admitted soon.

15. There's something about this business contract that doesn't seem right. I'm going to have my lawyer review it as I <u>smell a rat</u>.

16. Wanda's home cleaning business has become a real <u>cash cow</u> for her.

17. We don't have to fix the problem this way. There is <u>more than one way to skin a cat</u> and we're open to suggestions.

18. Why do you want to stir up trouble again between those old enemies? Can't you <u>let sleeping dogs lie</u>?

19. They went to a new laundromat that also serves coffee and bagels and <u>killed two birds with one stone</u>; they got clean clothes while they ate breakfast!

20. The company was worried about hiring a retired engineer but soon realized that you *can* <u>teach an old dog new tricks</u>.

21. Don't you understand? Zoë decided to apply for the same job as you just to <u>get</u> your <u>goat</u>.

22. Brad only looks threatening. He would <u>not hurt a fly</u>.

23. Jaime expected to be promoted easily, but learned that a <u>dark horse</u> from another department is also being considered for that opening.

24. You can see the town of Chesterfield across the lake. It's about twelve miles <u>as the crow flies</u>, but almost ninety miles by car.

25. Are you afraid to ask LaDonna for help? Don't worry, her <u>bark is worse than</u> her <u>bite</u>. She'll be glad to help you.

Answer key for Every Body Idioms Exercise – Section 1

1. Adina had a lot of work to finish by the end of the day and asked if I could <u>lend</u> her <u>a hand</u> to get it all done.

2. My stapler disappeared yesterday and today my note pad is gone. Someone in this office has <u>sticky fingers</u>.

3. The copier machine in the office is <u>on its last legs</u>. We'll have to get a new one soon.

4. I'll have to <u>bone up on</u> the latest statistics before I give that presentation on Monday.

5. Can we meet <u>face to face</u> to discuss this new project?

6. Kenzo didn't want to go out to dinner, but we <u>twisted</u> his <u>arm</u> and made him come with us.

7. Because his new assistant was still <u>wet behind the ears</u>, the electrician had to rewire the house by himself.

8. Lionel got <u>cold feet</u> and didn't propose marriage to his girl-friend Saturday night as he had planned.

9. That song is <u>getting on</u> my <u>nerves</u>. Could you turn down the radio please?

10. The folder you've been looking for is <u>right under</u> your <u>nose</u>.

11. Oh, we're late! We'll have to <u>shake a leg</u> if we want to get to the movie on time.

12. Zeljko <u>fought tooth and nail</u> for sole custody of his child.

13. Tibor and Ed have disagreed about this situation for a long time and will never <u>see eye to eye</u> about it.

14. Let's <u>keep</u> our <u>fingers</u> crossed that our company gets that new contract and we keep our jobs.

15. What a good worker Joe is. He's here every day, <u>nose to the grindstone</u>, quietly doing his job.

16. Meg is <u>head over heels</u> about the young man she met six months ago at your party.

17. We've been planning to redecorate our kitchen for a while now. I can't wait to <u>sink</u> my <u>teeth into</u> it this weekend.

18. Why is Nick <u>giving</u> me <u>the cold shoulder</u>? Is he mad at me for something?

19. If no money <u>changed hands</u>, the car was a gift.

20. Carlo is used to ignoring his wife's endless complaints. They go <u>in one ear and out the other</u>.

21. Paulina gets anything she wants from her parents; she has them both <u>wrapped around</u> her <u>finger</u>.

22. When Taddeus met his girlfriend's parents for the first time, he <u>put</u> his <u>best foot forward</u> to impress them.

23. Simon is making money <u>hand over fist</u> at his new job on Wall Street.

24. Don't get your <u>nose out of joint</u> just because I don't want to go with you to your mother's this weekend.

25. Did you really win the lottery or are you <u>pulling</u> my <u>leg</u>?

26. When he addressed the long-haired young man at the counter as "Miss," Giorgio <u>put</u> his <u>foot in</u> his <u>mouth</u>.

27. I'm not sure what we're doing after the game on Saturday. Let's <u>play it by ear</u> then, ok?

28. Nell was very tempted to tell Andy what she thought of him, but she <u>bit</u> her <u>tongue</u> and kept quiet.

Answer key for Every Body Idioms Exercise – Section 2

29. Sal tries to fix things around the house, but he is <u>all</u> <u>thumbs</u>.

30. You can't continue to <u>turn a blind eye to</u> your son's bad behavior in school.

31. Serena thought Milly was her best friend until Milly <u>stabbed</u> her <u>in the back</u> and stole her boyfriend.

32. I don't want anyone to know what we're planning, so <u>keep</u> your <u>mouth shut</u> about it.

33. Oliver <u>paid through the nose</u> for that gold watch. He could have bought it for much less at another store.

34. Watch this. I'm going to <u>bust</u> Tom's <u>chops</u> about his missing that shot in the game this afternoon.

35. Caleb is a great worker and <u>pulls</u> his <u>weight</u> on every project.

36. If you <u>use</u> your <u>head / noggin / noodle / nut</u>, you can figure out how to save more money each month.

37. The meeting with my ex-husband's lawyer was very unpleasant and <u>left a bad taste in</u> my <u>mouth</u>.

38. Whenever we go out to dinner, Al complains about everything. Why does he have to be such <u>a pain in the neck</u>?

39. Since getting out of jail, Devon has <u>kept</u> his <u>nose clean</u> and is working hard at his job.

40. I'm not going to <u>stick</u> my <u>neck out</u> and complain if the rest of you aren't going to do it with me.

41. Maggie's an <u>old hand</u> at real estate. She'll help you sell your house and find you a new one to buy.

42. I've never gone snowboarding, but I'm going to <u>get</u> my <u>feet wet</u> and try it this weekend at that local resort.

43. You won't solve your problems unless you stop <u>burying</u> your <u>head in the sand</u> and face them.

44. Buy the sweater or not. It's <u>no skin off</u> my <u>nose</u> either way!

45. If you're so upset with him, why don't you <u>give</u> Neal <u>a piece of</u> your <u>mind</u>?

46. You may think you're right about this issue, but you don't have <u>a leg to stand on</u>.

47. Raising children today is not easy, <u>make no bones about it</u>.

48. Stay away from that guy. He walks around with a <u>chip on</u> his <u>shoulder</u> and is always looking for a fight.

49. The salesman kept insisting he would give me a good deal, but after awhile I realized it was just <u>lip service</u>.

50. Because Lidia refused to help her brother settle their late mother's estate, getting her inheritance was delayed. Just another case of her <u>cutting off</u> her <u>nose to spite</u> her <u>face</u>.

51. Would I like to eat some scorpions? <u>Not on your life</u>, thanks all the same.

52. The audience was <u>all ears</u> when the famous poet began to read from his latest book.

53. Did you see the ticket price on that Broadway show? It costs <u>an arm and a leg</u>!

54. I know you don't like Martin, but don't let him <u>get under</u> your <u>skin</u>.

55. Things are tough at home now, but, <u>keep</u> your <u>chin up</u>. Everything will get better soon.

Answer key for Get in on the Action Exercise

1. Lou is a good fair boss, but he <u>runs a tight ship</u> and expects everyone to follow the rules.

2. Make those payments on your credit card or you will soon be <u>behind the eight ball</u> and owe even more money.

3. Please don't give me another <u>song and dance</u> about why you are late for work again today.

4. Those of us who are unemployed are <u>in the same boat</u> when it comes to trying to put food on the table for our families.

5. Bill is pretty tough. No matter how bad things get at work or at home he always seems to <u>roll with the punches</u>.

6. The judging at Saturday night's dance contest <u>came down to the wire</u>. Paul and Tatiana managed to win by one vote.

7. I have no interest in deep sea fishing, but when my friends planned a trip, I decided to <u>go along for the ride</u> as it was a nice day to be out on the ocean.

8. Walt hid his illness for months, but it's impossible to <u>sweep</u> that kind of thing <u>under the rug</u> for long.

9. I'm happy to know it's been <u>smooth sailing</u> for them since they brought their new baby home from the hospital.

10. Writing books was one thing; promoting them in book stores and on TV was a <u>whole new ball game</u> for the author.

11. Sheila was disappointed to learn that she was <u>out of the running</u> for the grand prize in the quilting competition.

12. Before this problem can be settled, everyone has to <u>put</u> their <u>cards on the table</u> so we all know where we stand.

13. Kevin has bought many used cars, so he is a good person to take with you for advice as he <u>knows the ropes</u>.

14. That was rather mean of Angela to criticize your new hairdo. It's not like her to <u>hit below the belt</u> like that.

15. Please don't <u>make waves</u> at Aunt Prita's birthday party by reminding her that she owes us money.

16. Yay! My favorite boutique just opened a new store <u>a hop, skip, and a jump</u> away from my house!

17. Bonita is <u>skating on thin ice</u> at work as she never gets her work done on time.

18. There are only five waiters here tonight for dinner service, so they will all need to track their orders and to be <u>on the ball</u>.

19. Louisa helps at the animal shelter as she <u>gets a kick</u> <u>out of</u> walking the dogs and playing with the cats while they await adoption.

20. Told you to ask her out. Now Jim's dating her and you, my friend, have <u>missed the boat</u> again.

21. Who knows the future? I don't know what's <u>in the cards</u> for me next year and neither do you.

22. It was <u>sink or swim</u> time for the young company when, after months of preparation, it launched its first website.

23. This is the fifth time we've had to discipline you this year for poor work. For the last time, <u>shape up or ship out</u>.

24. You've worked so hard for your degree. Don't <u>throw in the towel</u> now that you're almost finished.

25. Let the buyer make an offer first. Don't <u>jump the gun</u> and give him a price that might be lower than what he's willing to pay.

26. Peter loves to <u>rock the boat</u> at town hall meetings by asking challenging questions.

27. In order to get this sales contract, I will have to <u>play ball</u> with Renaldo, whom I dislike intensely.

Answer key for Economic Idioms Exercise

1. That's a beautiful leather coat. I'll bet it cost you <u>a pretty penny</u>.

2. Thanks for picking me up when my car broke down today. <u>I owe you one.</u>

3. Karl asked us to lend him a thousand dollars, but since he never repaid his last loan, we told him <u>nothing doing.</u>

4. Want to make a <u>fast buck</u>? Deliver these printed samples to the City and I'll pay you $25 cash when you get back.

5. Her mom's all-time favorite singer was Nat King Cole, <u>no two ways about it.</u>

6. You can easily find those plain window blinds in any hardware store. They're <u>a dime a dozen</u> and nothing special.

7. Don't be afraid to go snorkeling. It's easy. Believe me, there's <u>nothing to it.</u>

8. Sanjay's becoming a millionaire after such humble beginnings is a very inspiring <u>rags-to-riches</u> story.

9. I don't know which house painter we should hire. They're both professional and not too expensive, so <u>six of one, half dozen of another</u>, pick either one.

10. Glad to see you finally <u>put two and two together</u> and figured out that Sammo is not your friend.

11. Come on, I'll treat you to lunch. I know you've been <u>pinching pennies</u> lately.

12. Paying the cable bill was your responsibility and you forgot. Don't <u>pass the buck</u> and blame it on me.

13. Eric has to take a Japanese literature class in order to get his degree, but his college no longer offers that course. What a <u>catch-22</u>.

14. Sergio will <u>stop at nothing</u> to get Sophia to marry him.

15. Lex is a good friend. He knows how to listen, but doesn't <u>put in</u> his <u>two cents</u> unless I ask him for his advice.

16. Susan and James always intended to <u>save for a rainy day</u>, but somehow they never did.

17. Luis is working too hard lately. <u>Dollars to doughnuts</u> it's going to catch up to him very soon.

18. I'm asking you to <u>think twice</u> before contributing any money to his cause.

19. Antonio has never directed a movie before? Oh great! <u>Here goes nothing</u>.

Answer key for Worldly Goods Idioms Exercise

1. Ray's going to walk barefoot across the entire country. He's not <u>off his rocker</u> though; he's raising money for charity.

2. Considering that you owe her a thousand dollars, giving her ten dollars is barely <u>a drop in the bucket</u>.

3. Gloria <u>hit the nail on the head</u> when she guessed that Reggie would propose to Emily on her birthday.

4. I'll share my secret with you if you promise to keep it <u>under your hat</u> until I tell you otherwise.

5. If Alexandra is late for work one more time, she's going to get the ax.

6. I'm still on the fence about whether to paint the bedroom dark gray or a pale blue.

7. He'll pay you under the table if you help him remove that junk from the school basement.

8. I'm having such a terrible day. I feel like I got up on the wrong side of the bed this morning.

9. Beth asked if she could drive my new Mercedes to Reno and I told her, "No soap."

10. Theo just learned that his young daughter needs another expensive operation. Let's pass the hat for him this week.

11. The sellers thought they had each of us over a barrel because we were both interested in buying their house. But I found another house that I liked better and bought that one.

12. Don't get so hot under the collar, pal. No one is bothering your girlfriend.

13. Please call me before nine tonight. I'm planning to hit the hay early and get a good night's sleep.

14. Pam's friends were shocked that she was dating someone ten years younger; however, Pam evidently doesn't mind robbing the cradle.

15. You can't believe what Marita might tell you about her experiences working in Hollywood. She has a tendency to <u>talk through</u> her <u>hat</u>.

16. That company had me fill out tons of forms, take several tests, and generally <u>put</u> me <u>through the wringer</u>. Then they didn't hire me!

17. Iris decided to go <u>on the wagon</u> for a few months in an effort to lose more weight.

18. You'd better slow down. You've been <u>burning the candle at both ends</u> for the past six months, and you're going to regret it soon, trust me.

19. They bought the house as well as everything in it, <u>lock, stock and barrel</u>.

20. The deal they offered you is not very good. In my opinion, if you put your money into it, you'll <u>lose</u> your <u>shirt</u>.

21. Lester <u>hit the roof</u> when the final bill for his son's dental work came in yesterday's mail.

22. Rachel was about to tell John that she didn't want to date him any longer when he <u>turned the tables</u> on her and told her the same thing.

23. Relax man! We're almost there. <u>Keep</u> your <u>shirt on</u>!

24. When he worked in the movie theater, Diego <u>wore many / several hats</u>: he sold the tickets, ran the snack concession, showed the movies, and cleaned up the theater every night.

Answer key for It's Only Natural Idioms Exercise

1. Tell me exactly what's on your mind and don't <u>beat around the bush</u>.

2. We won't go to the mall on Saturday if you're still feeling <u>under the weather</u>.

3. When the company suddenly closed, its 90 employees were left <u>high and dry</u> with no income and no health insurance.

4. Running a dog grooming salon was <u>a walk in the park</u> for Kendra compared to working at the veterinarian's office.

5. Variel <u>runs hot and cold</u> when it comes to José; one day she is in love with him and the next day, she isn't.

6. Adam's parents remained at the hospital after their infant son's surgery until he was completely <u>out of the woods</u>.

7. Clark has been working <u>day in and day out</u> to find new homes for the orphaned children.

8. Dennis <u>slept like a log</u> last night after biking 25 miles yesterday afternoon.

9. Do you think that when Francine gets out of jail she will <u>turn over a new leaf</u> and lead a better life?

10. When Will and Robin decided to divorce, they <u>fought fire with fire</u> to get what each wanted in the final judgment.

11. Go ahead. Offer to buy that woman a drink just to <u>break the ice</u> and see if she'll talk to you.

12. Eva's comment about my crooked teeth was <u>the last straw</u>. I'm not going to forgive her for her insults anymore.

13. Some choice. Hector can start working the overnight shift at the factory next month or keep working days and take a 15% pay cut. He's caught <u>between a rock and a hard place</u>.

14. That Cosmo is <u>full of hot air</u>. It's not possible that he went lion hunting in Africa last week.

15. I'll be <u>in hot water</u> with my parents if I don't get at least a C in math this semester.

16. Working with both the workers' union and management was <u>no bed of roses</u> but a new contract was finally agreed upon.

Answer key for Rainbow Idioms Exercise

1. They've only been dating for a month, so Marco's marriage proposal to Leann came <u>out of the blue</u>.

2. Frank's work habits are so poor, he must have several <u>black marks</u> against him.

3. Is Gareth getting ill? He looks a bit <u>green around the gills</u>.

4. They've been <u>in the red</u> for many months, but with Tao's new job, they can start paying down their debts.

5. Emil needs to be challenged to use more of his <u>gray matter</u> so he can improve as a student.

6. You can tell her to save money until you are <u>blue in the face</u>. If she doesn't want to do it, she won't.

7. C'mon. I'm tired of staying home all the time. Let's go out tonight and <u>paint the town red</u> for a change.

8. He thought that owning a car wash would be <u>a gold mine</u>, but it didn't earn as much money as he had hoped.

9. We are just waiting to get <u>the green light</u> from you so we can start renovating your kitchen.

10. Nardo gambled away all his money and is bankrupt. For him to criticize his brother for playing poker with his friends is <u>the pot calling the kettle black</u>.

11. We had to wade through a ton of <u>red tape</u> before we could get the business registered in the state's vendor database.

12. They were happy to hear that Melissa is back <u>in the pink</u> after her bicycle accident.

13. Generally, they don't eat fast food, but, <u>once in a blue moon</u> they'll stop for a hamburger and some fries.

14. No one knew who was vandalizing the classrooms until Mrs. Brown <u>caught</u> a student <u>red-handed</u>.

15. Every time Yasuo talks about his first wife, his second wife <u>sees red</u>.

Answer key for Grab Bag Idioms Exercise – Section 1

1. Paul completely <u>missed the point</u> of what the doctor was telling him about his chemotherapy treatments.

2. You'll be better off <u>in the long run</u> if you try to save some money each month.

3. Lynn's boss <u>bent over backwards</u> to help her when she was having health problems.

4. The three friends got some unexpected cash and decided to go to Las Vegas and <u>live it up</u>.

5. Boyd has <u>cut down on</u> his alcohol consumption since he became ill.

6. Those two have been working together for so many years that they are <u>on the same wavelength</u>.

7. Ray disliked his daughter's boyfriend right <u>from the get-go</u>.

8. When Jun Fai volunteered to head the committee, Shannon was glad she was <u>off the hook</u> and wouldn't have to do it.

9. The paper arrived <u>in the nick of time</u> and we were able to print the presentation notes before the meeting started.

10. Masha was delighted to hear from her cousin Pavel as they had been <u>out of touch</u> for years.

11. He sold his stamp collection, went to a casino, and, <u>easy come, easy go</u>, lost all the money at the blackjack table.

12. Everyone in this group was working well together until the boss told us to include Dan. Why couldn't she <u>leave well enough alone</u>?

13. If you have teenage children, it's a good idea to <u>keep tabs on</u> where they are going and whom they are seeing.

14. Don't worry if you don't do it right the first time. Just <u>give it</u> your <u>best shot</u> and that will be fine.

15. Zach ran out of his cold medicine late last night. He was <u>in luck</u> though, as the pharmacy is open 24 hours and he was able to get more.

16. All their plans to move to Costa Rico went <u>down the drain</u> when they lost all their money.

17. Oh no, this list of names is <u>out of order</u> and now I have to retype the whole thing.

18. Walter was <u>sick and tired</u> of his boring life and longed for some excitement.

19. We've been painting since early this morning and I'm exhausted. Let's <u>call it a day</u> and have some dinner.

20. Anita puts so much effort into trying to <u>keep up with the Joneses</u> even though she already has plenty.

21. The people next door had a very loud party last night and we <u>didn't sleep a wink</u>.

22. Fred's been avoiding speaking with his elderly parents about their finances, but he has to <u>bite the bullet</u> and do it soon.

23. I'm sorry about arguing with you at work last week. I hope there are <u>no hard feelings</u>.

Answer key for Grab Bag Idioms Exercise – Section 2

24. The store didn't have the exact color thread I wanted so I bought something close that should <u>do the trick</u>.

25. You can <u>play dumb</u>, but everyone knows you were involved in getting Dennis fired.

26. The principal called the three students into her office to <u>get to the bottom of</u> their constant fighting.

27. Gregory has agreed not to notify the police if his missing money is returned by tomorrow, <u>no questions asked</u>.

28. Silvain often bragged about being a great goalie. He certainly <u>changed</u> his <u>tune</u> last night after his team lost the game.

29. What is Bianca going to do to <u>make ends meet</u> until she can get another job?

30. The company claimed there would be no layoffs next month. The workers <u>read between the lines</u> and suspected otherwise.

31. Passing the tests to get into graduate school was <u>no picnic</u>, but Lorenzo was glad he had done it.

32. That real estate agent is <u>on a roll</u> this month. She has sold two houses and listed three more.

33. As everyone is very busy today, I'll make this announcement <u>short and sweet</u> so we can all get right back to work.

34. Several students were suspected of inciting the riots, but it was hard to determine which one was <u>calling the shots</u>.

35. Melinda has been avoiding seeing a doctor about the mole on her back. She needs to <u>face the music</u> and make an appointment right away.

36. We're very busy, but please <u>sit tight</u> and someone will help you in a moment.

37. I absolutely have to complete this project by next Tuesday, <u>no ifs, ands, or buts</u>.

38. Since getting a pay raise, Ti Hua has been able to get <u>out from under</u> most of his bills.

39. Luther's sculpture has to be finished in time for an exhibit in two months. The next several weeks will be <u>all work and no play</u> for him.

40. Does Halle really expect to get an invitation to the royal wedding? <u>Fat chance</u>!

41. Tanya loves to buy clothes. This past month alone she has bought <u>more</u> sweaters <u>than</u> you <u>can shake a stick at</u>.

42. Neither the president nor the cabinet seems to know what to do in this crisis. It's like <u>the blind leading the blind</u> in our government right now.

43. Rudy is tired of worrying about his sister's marital problems and is not going to <u>lose sleep over</u> them any more.

44. Mr. and Mrs. Roth's bagel store was doing very well until they doubled its size. Now, sales are the same but their costs are greater. They should have <u>quit while</u> they <u>were ahead</u>.

45. Emilio always offers to help his friends, but it's usually <u>too little, too late</u> because he's not really sincere.

46. Martin volunteered to lead this investigation, but he has <u>bitten off more than</u> he <u>can chew</u> and is struggling with his duties.

Answer key for Grab Bag Idioms Exercise – Section 3

47. Wasn't losing that race in front of her friends enough of a disappointment for Laura? Do you have to <u>rub it in</u> with <u>a cheap shot</u> too?

48. Don't expect a <u>fair shake</u> if Charles is your opponent. He is determined to win <u>by hook or by crook</u>.

49. I hate it when Veronica and Kazuko argue. I <u>draw the line</u> at <u>taking sides</u> when it comes to my friends.

50. Georgia's financial situation has <u>gone from bad to worse</u>. She can't pay her bills this month and does<u>n't know where to turn</u> for help.

51. Last year, Natasha's son kept getting into trouble in school. She <u>laid down the law</u> with him and now he is <u>on the right track</u>.

52. Kiho thought the seller was <u>on the level</u> but he should have known the price on that condo was <u>too good to be true</u>.

53. This morning, Shirley said that the copy machine was <u>out of order</u> and <u>no sooner said than done</u>, it was repaired.

54. Although he had only one more year of studies to complete for his degree, Luke <u>lost sight of</u> why he wanted to be an engineer and decided to <u>call it quits</u>.

55. "<u>Believe it or not</u>, Jorge won the mega jackpot lottery twice in one year." "<u>No kidding</u>!"

56. Getting all this work done before Friday is <u>a tall order</u>, but it's not <u>out of the question</u>.

57. Those two friends have been <u>through thick and thin</u> together and have always been <u>fair and square</u> with each other.

58. Sharon has never liked Will. Something about him <u>rubs</u> her <u>the wrong way</u> and there's <u>no way</u> she'd ever agree to work with him again.

59. Hey! Mr. <u>Johnny-come-lately</u>! You criticize everything we do after it's done. Why don't you <u>put up or shut up</u>?

59. Hiring an assistant sounded like a good idea to Ross, but his new employee has begun <u>giving</u> him <u>a hard time</u> about the long hours she is expected to work. <u>Live and learn</u>, right?

Live and Learn! – *Basic* American Idioms *for* ESL Students

Index

Index

127